Be a Zillionaire

The Young Zillionaire's Guide to Buying Goods and Services

Tom Ridgway

the rosen publishing group's
rosen
central

To SW, RG, and AB for their support, and especially to SM for her unending patience.

Published in 2000 by The Rosen Publishing Group, Inc.
29 East 21st Street, New York, NY 10010

First Edition

Library of Congress Cataloging-in-Publication Data

Ridgway, Tom.
    The young zillionaire's guide to buying goods and services / Tom Ridgway.
      p.   cm. — (Be a zillionaire)
    Includes bibliographical references and index.
    Summary: Provides information on the basics of buying goods and services and the role of goods and services in the economy.
    ISBN 0-8239-3263-X
    1. Purchasing—Juvenile literature. [1. Purchasing.] I. Title. II. Series.
    HF5437 .R46 2000
    640.42—dc21   00-027207

Manufactured in the United States of America

17.95

TABLE OF CONTENTS

Get Informed!

Believe it or not, this is a book about shopping. You might call it a travel guide to the mall. Maybe you don't think you need it. Perhaps you are sure that you know everything there is to know about shopping. After all, you do it every day. But shopping involves more than just buying stuff. Shopping is really all about decision making. And you can make good decisions only when you have all the information you need.

Shopping is more than simply buying things because it is actually a vital part of the economy. Think of the economy as a big circular chain. Shopping is a link in the chain, and it joins up with other parts of the economy. So shopping links to banks, which link to businesses, which link to the govern-ment (through taxes), which links to consumers (that's you), who link with stores, which link with shopping, which links with banks, which link with businesses . . . and on we go. Some of these links are stronger than others, but each is just as important as the others in its own way. If one part of the chain is weak, it affects all the others. Holding this chain together is money—dollars and cents, pesos and pounds, yuan and yen.

Another reason that shopping is more than simply buying stuff is that we live in a world of limited resources. When you buy goods and services, you are consuming—that is, using up resources. If resources were unlimited, there would be no need to think twice about shopping. You could just go out and buy anything you wanted, when you wanted. But we can't do this in today's world. We have to choose wisely when we buy. And choosing wisely is impossible if we don't have all the facts we need to make an informed decision.

As you're reading this book, think about ways that having more information could have saved you money in the past and how it can help you save in the future. Look back at how you spent your money, say, in the last week, and see if you might have done it differently if you had had more information. The great thing about being armed with information is that it puts you—not big companies, not teachers or parents, but you—in control. And there is no better feeling than controlling your own future.

Goods and Services

What are goods and services? A good is a thing, a product that physically exists, like a pair of shoes, a bottle of nail polish, or a box of popcorn. A service is something that doesn't physically exist but that is bought and sold. For example, when you buy an airline ticket or pay a company to hook up your computer to the Internet, you are purchasing the assistance of the airline representative or Internet service provider.

Economists often call a service an "intangible good." This means that a service is a good that you can't touch. And that's a handy way of remembering the difference. You can touch a computer (a good), but you can't actually touch an Internet service provider (a service, as the name suggests).

You Can't Always Get What You Want

In a world of limited resources, not everyone can have everything that they want. That may seem obvious, but it is a central idea to economists. It means that everything has a price and a cost. When economists talk about the price of a good or a service, they usually mean how much money it takes to obtain the good or service.

Cost involves more than that. The cost of a good or service is what you give up to get it, the value of what you can't have or do because you chose something else instead. Economists call this the opportunity cost. Think of it this way:

You have fifty cents in your pocket and you are hungry and thirsty. But with fifty cents, you can only buy either a hot dog *or* a soda. You decide that you are more thirsty than hungry, so you choose to buy the soda. But buying the soda, of course, means that you can't buy the hot dog. The cost of your purchase is the hot dog—you gave up your chance to have it when you decided to buy the soda instead.

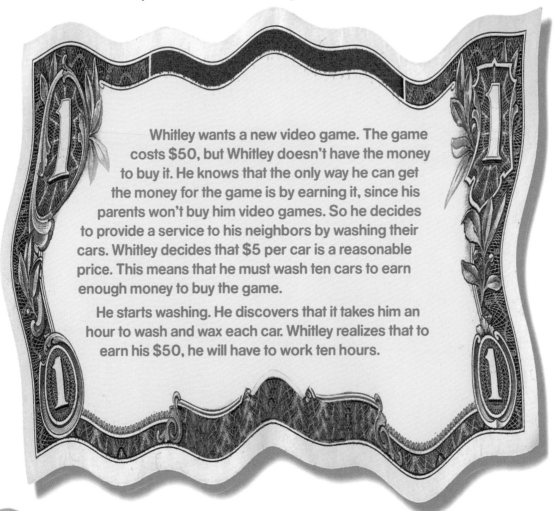

Whitley wants a new video game. The game costs $50, but Whitley doesn't have the money to buy it. He knows that the only way he can get the money for the game is by earning it, since his parents won't buy him video games. So he decides to provide a service to his neighbors by washing their cars. Whitley decides that $5 per car is a reasonable price. This means that he must wash ten cars to earn enough money to buy the game.

He starts washing. He discovers that it takes him an hour to wash and wax each car. Whitley realizes that to earn his $50, he will have to work ten hours.

So what is Whitley's cost? The video game has a price of fifty dollars—that's how much money it takes to buy the game. But the cost of the game is not simply fifty dollars. For Whitley, the cost is the ten hours he spends washing cars.

To Spend or Not to Spend

Every time you decide whether you want to buy a good or a service, you, like Whitley, must make a simple economic decision: Is the price worth the cost? In Whitley's case, does the game have more value than all the other things he could do during those ten hours? This might include reading a book or playing soccer with friends. For Whitley, the answer is yes.

By the way, cost doesn't have to be another good or service that must be given up. It can be something as simple as your time. Even so, it's still an economic decision. Whitley placed more value on the game than on any other activity he could have participated in while he was washing cars, and he valued the game more than any other good he could have bought with the fifty dollars he earned.

Cost, Price, and Resources

The cost of a good or service should reflect (in theory at least) the amount of resources used to make it. For example, a car is much more expensive than a bicycle because more parts are needed to make a car than a bike, meaning that more raw materials are used. In addition, more time is spent

putting car parts together than bike parts, so more money is needed to pay autoworkers than bike makers.

The same idea applies to a service: The cost of a service is reflected in the wages of people who work for the company, or in the goods that have to be bought in order to provide the service, such as airplanes for an airline. So it can be said that the price of a good or a service is a reflection of its cost.

This cost is then passed on to the consumer, who must work harder and longer to pay for goods and services that cost more. Because it takes more resources to build a car than a bike, buying a car will cost more than buying a bike. You will have to work much more to buy a car than to buy a bicycle. In other words, your cost—the number of hours you must work to earn enough money, for example—will be higher for the car. And cost, as well as its reflection—price—are both measured in money.

Bartering

Before people had money, they used to barter things. Bartering means that you exchange one good or service for another. People used to barter all sorts of things—vegetables, wool, and meat, for example.

In the Trobriand Islands in the Pacific Ocean, people used to barter for goods and services with yams. One yam might equal two fish; fifty yams might equal mending the roof of a house. Bartering can get very complicated, however, so money was gradually introduced to simplify things. As you know, Whitley receives five dollars for every car he washes. But think about what it would be like if he got five yams instead. What would Whitley do if the store didn't want to exchange yams for a video game? (And let's not even think about having to carry a big sack of yams around every time you go shopping!)

Money simplifies the exchange of one good for another—and it's much easier to carry around. Whitley

washes cars, is given money, and then gives that money to the store to buy his game. In other words, he exchanges his service (washing cars) for money and then exchanges that money for a good—his game. And where is the money? It's in the middle of the exchange of goods and services. This is one reason why money is often called a medium of exchange—"medium" comes from the Latin word for "middle."

Money also simplifies things because it makes comparing the prices, and thus the cost, of things much easier. It might be hard for Whitley to remember that five yams equal one washed car, which equals one hour of work, which equals a tenth of a computer game. Money makes it simpler by making exchanges more transparent, or clear.

Using money also means that you can compare things that are not alike; for example, you can compare the price of a bicycle with the price of a bottle of water. Whitley's purchase was made much simpler by money. He simply looked at the price of the game and worked out how long he would have to work in order to earn the money to buy it.

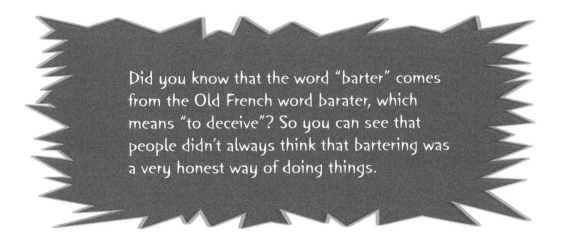

Did you know that the word "barter" comes from the Old French word barater, which means "to deceive"? So you can see that people didn't always think that bartering was a very honest way of doing things.

This Money's Not for Burning!

Since most of us have limited resources, it is best to be careful how we use them. Decisions about how to use them need to be carefully thought out.

Making a Budget

Before you buy anything, even something small, you must know how much money you have and can spend. To do that, you must make a budget.

The best way to start making a budget is to create a spending plan. Draw two columns on a piece of paper. At the top of one column, write "Income," and at the top of the other, "Expenses." To figure out your income, write down all the money you receive each week. This might be money you earn doing chores, your allowance, or money that you've already saved. Then total up that money.

INCOME		EXPENSES	
$10	(allowance from parents)	$1.50	(sodas)
$5	(mowing lawn)	$4	(magazines)
$15	(washing cars)	$5.50	(bus fares)
$5	(walking dogs)	$6	(pizza, ice cream)
		$5.29	(school supplies)
		$7	(movie ticket)
		$6	(pager subscription)

TOTALS

$35	$35.29

Difference: 29¢ more expenses than income

Now think about what you usually spend in a week—these are your expenses. They might include bus fare to school, lunch, or a trip to the movies. Don't forget to include little things such as candy or soda. Then total all the money you spend and compare your income with your expenses. If you have a higher figure on the income side than on the expense side, then you receive more money than you spend. That's good news! But if the amount is higher in the expenses column, you spend more than you receive. That means just one thing: *It's budget time!*

Start Saving

First, think about how you can cut your expenses. Make another table, but this time label one column "Needs" and the other "Wants." In the Needs column, write down your fixed expenses—the things that you must spend money on, no matter what. In the Wants column, write down the things that you want but could live without. Think carefully about this. Do you need popcorn every time you see a movie or the extra slice of pizza you always seem to buy? See how much you can save each week by not buying these things.

Before you start moaning and groaning, here's the good news: Just because you decide that the popcorn and pizza are extras doesn't mean that you can never have these things. The idea is to cut down, not out.

Impulse Buying, or I Want That!

Have you noticed that candy is always next to the cash register in supermarkets? There is a reason for that. Usually you go to the supermarket to buy necessities—like a quart of milk—but while you are waiting in line, you see the candy. Maybe you hadn't thought about candy until that moment, but you decide to buy a candy bar anyway. Surprise! You've fallen into the trap that the store set for you. You have impulse bought.

When people impulse buy, they don't stop to think about what they are buying. They just see and buy.

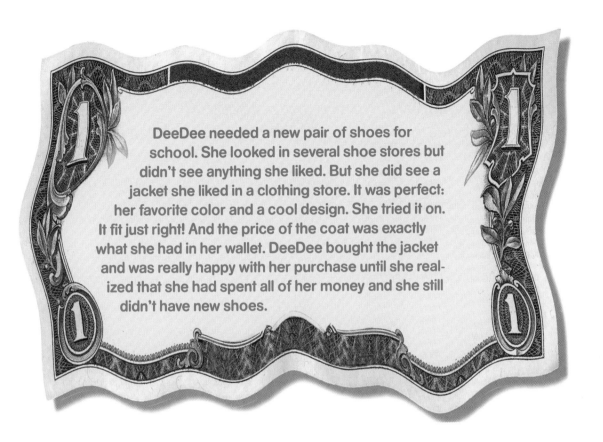

DeeDee needed a new pair of shoes for school. She looked in several shoe stores but didn't see anything she liked. But she did see a jacket she liked in a clothing store. It was perfect: her favorite color and a cool design. She tried it on. It fit just right! And the price of the coat was exactly what she had in her wallet. DeeDee bought the jacket and was really happy with her purchase until she realized that she had spent all of her money and she still didn't have new shoes.

Impulse buying is the worst possible way to shop because you buy without planning and often without having enough information about the product you are buying. Experts estimate that young people waste $20 billion a year by making bad impulse buys! To make the most of your money, you must think ahead.

Perhaps thinking ahead about your purchases seems a little silly. After all, buying a soda may not seem like a big purchase. But think about it. Let's say that you spend

50¢ on a soda every day. Multiply that by 365 (the number of days in a year) and you'll see that you are spending $182.50 a year on soda alone. That's $182.50 you could save just by drinking from a water fountain! Remember, it is not the price but the cost that matters, and the cost is all the other things you could have bought with all the money you spent on sodas—like a bunch of new CDs, a bike, or a new jacket.

Get Rich!

Now that you've started to save a little more of the money you receive each week, it is time to look at ways to boost your income.

Negotiating Your Allowance

For many kids, the main source of money is the allowance they receive from their parents. This is a set amount that your parents give you regularly so that you can be in charge of your own money.

If you aren't receiving an allowance right now, you may want to ask your parents what they think of giving you one. Of course, you've got to do some preparation before you ask them. Make a spending plan to show them, think about what you're going to tell them, and try to show them that you will be responsible with the money they give you. Here are a few hints as to how you can impress your parents into seeing things your way.

How to Ask for an Allowance

 First of all, show your parents your spending plan and explain to them that letting you run your own budget is good practice for later, when you will have much larger responsibilities, such as credit cards and a mortgage.

 Tell them that according to experts, your allowance shouldn't be tied to your household chores. Thus as a member of the household, you will do your fair share of chores without being paid for them (that's sure to please them!). Suggest that perhaps you can earn extra money in addition to your allowance by doing special chores such as mowing the lawn or painting the fence.

 Ask your parents to put your allowance every month into a bank account that you will open (see chapter 5). That way it will be harder for you to get to the money and easier to avoid impulse buys. Plus, your parents won't have to remember every week to give you your allowance.

 Tell your parents that you plan to save a portion of your allowance each week. For example, maybe you'll put away 10 percent of your allowance every week to save up for a more expensive item or for schoolbooks.

 Tell them that you are willing to let them check now and then to see if you are spending your money wisely.

 Make sure that you and your parents agree on and are clear about what your allowance covers. Does it include clothes? Does it include school supplies, or is it just for fun things? It's better to deal with these questions now rather than let them become a problem later.

What If I Can't Get an Allowance?

Not everyone's parents can, or want to, give their children an allowance. If your parents don't think that they can or don't like the idea, think of other ways to

increase your income. There are lots of ways to make a little extra money, even if you're not old enough to get a real job. Think about what you're good at and what you enjoy doing. If you like being outside and working with your hands, maybe you could mow lawns, do some gardening, or paint houses, signs, and fences. If you love computers, you could try giving computer lessons to adults, though you should know that you will probably need to be very patient to do this. There are lots of different ways to make your income grow. All it takes is imagination and a willingness to work.

Above all, be realistic when determining how much of an allowance you ask for from your parents. Remember that your parents are more likely to agree if you ask for a sensible amount. You'll have a much better chance for success if you ask for ten dollars than if you ask for fifty.

Research, Compare, Save

Now that you've started saving and have your budget in order, you are well equipped to head out to shop. This chapter shows you how to shop smart!

Smart Shopping

The first rule of smart shopping is to really think about whether you want the product. Ask yourself why you want it, what makes it so special to you, and if you think the product is a good value for the money. Ask yourself if you really want it for yourself or just because your friends have it.

Once you are sure that you want the item, the next step is to go comparison shopping. Visit at least three stores that carry the product that you want and check the price at each store. Ask sales assistants if they would recommend the product; if not, what would they recommend instead? If any of your friends have the same product, ask them if they find it worth owning.

Research, Research, Research!

Of course, you can always let other people do some of the hard work for you. Take a look at *Consumer Reports* magazine, which is in many public libraries as well as most bookstores and magazine stands. *Consumer Reports* has tested thousands of different products and rated them for quality and value for the money. The magazine also has a Web site (*http://www.consumerreports.org*), where you can find reviews of many types of products.

In addition, *Consumer Reports* publishes a kids' magazine called *Zillions* that offers reviews of toys and games. The reviews are written not by adults but by young people like you. *Zillions* also has a Web site: *http://www.zillionsedcenter.org*. Another place to try is your local Better Business Bureau (BBB). It will have lots of information to help you choose the right product for you.

Sometimes price isn't the only thing you have to think about. If you are shopping for something such as a CD player or a computer, you should think about the warranty. A warranty is a guarantee to the customer that the product is free from defects. It usually means that if something goes wrong with your purchase within a certain time period (usually a year), it will be repaired or replaced for free.

A warranty can be very important. Say there are two similar products, one slightly cheaper than the other. The cheaper product has a warranty of six months; the other, a warranty of two years. It may be worth paying a little extra to get the product with the longer warranty so that if anything does go wrong, it will cost you nothing to have it repaired or replaced.

Don't forget to ask about return policies. Even with all of your research, you may purchase an item that is not exactly what you want. Some stores will return your money, but often you have to bring the item back within a certain period of time, such as thirty days. Other stores will give you only store credit, which means you can spend the money only in that store. Some stores do not accept returned items at all.

Using the Internet

The Internet is a great way to comparison shop. There are Web sites that can compare prices for you. You type in the name of a product, and the site will search the Internet for the best price available and where you can find it. (See the For More Information section at the back of this book for the addresses of some of these sites.)

It can be even more important to comparison shop when buying on the Internet than when shopping in stores. Research has shown that there are huge differences in prices according to which on-line store you visit. Prices for the same CD can differ by as much as 50 percent at different sites, book prices can differ as much as 33 percent, and airline tickets as much as 28 percent.

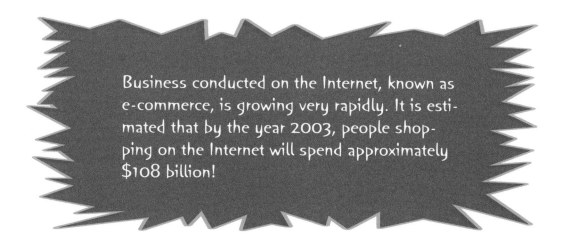

Business conducted on the Internet, known as e-commerce, is growing very rapidly. It is estimated that by the year 2003, people shopping on the Internet will spend approximately $108 billion!

The Internet is a great tool for research, but for young people there is one big problem: It is almost impossible to buy anything without a credit card! Fortunately, there are now sites that let you buy things without a credit card.

Here's how it works. You open an account and then get an adult to use his or her credit card to put money into your Web account. (The adult also has to sign up to say that he or she gives you permission to shop from that site.) The site has agreements with lots of different on-line stores, which accept the money from your account.

Whether you're shopping for a service or a good, and whether it's on the Internet or at the mall, the same rules apply. If you want to make the most of your money, there are three words to remember: research, research, research!

Work That Money!

You'll be working hard to earn your money. So while you're saving for your chosen product, make sure that your money works hard for you. The safest and simplest way to do this is to put it in a bank.

How Do Banks Work?

Banks are a vital link in the chain of the economy. When you deposit money in a bank, it's as if the bank is borrowing your money. Banks take the money deposited with them and lend it to businesses and individuals who need to borrow. This is called investment.

When a company wants to invest in, say, some new machinery, it goes to the bank. The bank lends it the money and charges it interest on the loan. Interest is the price that the company

has to pay in order to borrow the money the bank has collected from its depositors.

So what do you get out of the whole thing? Well, just as borrowers pay interest to the bank on the money that they borrow, the bank pays you interest in exchange for borrowing your money. The bank makes profits by charging customers more money—higher interest rates—to borrow money than it pays to people like you who deposit money. The difference between what the bank pays to depositors and how much interest it receives from borrowers is the bank's profit.

How Money Travels

Let's say that DeeDee learns from her impulse buy to think twice about spending and starts to plan a budget. She saves half of her allowance each week and works really hard. Her earnings grow and grow until she has $1,000. She goes to the bank and opens an account. The account pays an interest rate of 6 percent. In a year she has earned $60 in interest payments, giving her a total of $1,060. Her money has grown by $60 and she hasn't done anything!

Meanwhile, Lia needs a new oven for her coffee shop. She borrows $1,000 from the bank at an interest rate of 10 percent. After a year she has paid back the money plus $100 in interest payments, meaning she has paid a total of $1,100. The bank has made a profit of $40.

The cycle does not stop there. Remember that everything is linked together in a chain. Because of her new oven, Lia is able to serve more customers in her coffee shop and therefore makes more money. She puts that extra money into her bank account. The bank then gives this money to another business that needs a loan. This business then makes more money because of the new machinery (or whatever it bought with its loan), which the company deposits in the bank, which the bank lends to another business, which makes more money . . . and on it goes.

Saving, Spending, and the Economy

So you can see that saving helps the economy to work smoothly. It's like putting oil on a chain to make it stop squeaking. Normally, people save more money when the economy is good because they have more money to spare. When people save more, there is more money in the banking system, which means that it is cheaper to borrow money—interest rates are lower.

However, if the economy is not doing well, people save less, so there is less money in the banking system. This means that the price of money is higher because money is scarce—and interest rates are then higher. When interest rates are higher, people invest (borrow) less money because borrowing money is more expensive. But the higher interest rates encourage people to save. So as more people save, the price of money will go down again, since there will be more money to go around. And as the price goes down more, people will start to borrow money to invest, which will bring down interest rates again. This will help the economy as companies start to invest more again. It's that chain again!

So by saving, you aren't just earning money for yourself. You're also helping the economy to work better and allowing other people to make more money.

Shopping Around for a Bank

A bank is a service, and services should be chosen with as much care as goods. Do some research before choosing a bank. Visit banks in your area and ask about the different savings accounts they offer. When shopping for a bank account, keep the following things in mind.

Choosing a Bank

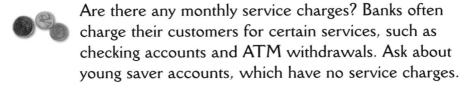

What rate of interest does the account pay? (Remember, you want the highest you can get.)

Are there any monthly service charges? Banks often charge their customers for certain services, such as checking accounts and ATM withdrawals. Ask about young saver accounts, which have no service charges.

Do you need to keep a minimum balance—that is, a minimum amount of money—in your account? Is there a fee if you drop below a certain amount? Try to find an account with no minimum balance.

Can you withdraw money whenever you want? With some savings accounts you have to tell the bank a few weeks or days in advance before you can withdraw your money.

Is the bank insured by the Federal Deposit Insurance Corporation (FDIC)? This government agency insures banks against bankruptcy. This means that your money is safe even if the bank goes out of business. Most banks are now FDIC insured, but you should check anyway.

Opening a Bank Account

Before you open an account, see if your parents have any tips about which bank to choose. Once you have decided on an account, a parent will have to come with you to sign a form (if you're under eighteen).

Once you open your account, you will receive either a passbook in which you keep track of your money or a monthly statement (sent by mail) telling you how much you have saved and how much interest you have earned. Store these documents in a safe place so that you can keep track of the money you have. That way you will always know how close you are to your goal. If you are saving up for a specific item, you can make a "savings-o-meter," a chart showing how close you are to your goal. Watching yourself get nearer and nearer to your goal may spur you on to save even faster!

Investing in Stocks and Shares

Another way to earn money on your savings is by investing in companies yourself. You can do this by buying stocks or shares. When you buy a share, you are actually buying a small part of a company. Shares are traded in special markets called stock markets. Most big cities have their own stock market—for example, in Paris it is called the Bourse (the French word for purse), and in New York it is commonly called Wall Street (the street where the market is based).

To make money, people buy shares in a company that they think will do well in the future. Say you buy shares in the CatSnacks Company for ten dollars each. The company then announces that it has made huge profits, and the price of each share goes up to twenty dollars. If you now sell your shares, you will make a profit of ten dollars on each share. If you hold lots of shares, that can add up to a lot of money.

But shares have one major disadvantage when compared with banks: Shares can go down as well as up. If CatSnacks announces that it has not made a big profit, the shares might go down. Maybe the ten dollar shares will go down to five dollars, meaning that the shares are worth half of what you paid for them. To get your money back, you have to keep your shares in the company until they rise again.

Before you launch yourself into the world of shares, it's a good idea to get some practice. There are Web sites that let you do this by trading on the real New York Stock

Exchange but with virtual (fake) money. (See the For More Information section of this book for addresses.)

As you can see, banks may not make you an instant zillionaire, but they won't put you in the poorhouse, either. The earnings on your savings might not be huge but you will never lose your money. Your savings can only go up. So for the moment, young zillionaires-in-training can practice their share dealing, but they should stick to banks to make their money work for them.

Burgernomics

The Internet isn't just a good way to go comparison shopping. It's also a great way to see what is going on in the world. Every year *The Economist*, a business magazine, compares the price of Big Macs all over the world. Why not start your own Web site (or add a section to your school's Web site) asking visitors to tell you how much a selection of products cost in their part of the world? Try to pick products that are available all over the world.

If you then convert these prices into dollars, you can see how much it costs to buy products around the world. (You can find currency conversion rates at many banks, in financial newspapers, on financial television programs, or on the Web.) You could also ask visitors what the equivalent of five dollars buys in their country. Not only is this a good way to learn about all the different currencies in the world, you might even find that it's cheaper to buy your chosen product on the other side of the world!

Advertising and Shopping for the Future

Just as companies and stores love impulse buys, they also love to try to persuade you to buy their products. To do this, they advertise.

How Do Advertisements Work?

An advertisement is a company's way of showing off its products. "Hey, you over there! Yes, you!" advertisements shout. "Look at me! Buy me!" In 1998, companies in the United States spent $79.5 billion on advertising their products. (Walt Disney alone spent $1.3 billion.) Out of these advertisements, 30,000 are aimed at kids every year. That's over eighty-two advertisements a day, which makes for a lot of shouting!

Using the Media

To help them get their message across, companies use the media. Just as money acts as a medium of exchange for goods and services, so radio, television, magazines, newspapers, billboards, and all the other places you see advertisements act as a medium for advertising goods and services. (The plural of medium is *media*—that's Latin again. The media is what we call television, the radio, newspapers, magazines, and the Internet.)

There's only one reason why companies want you to take notice: They want you to buy their products. And the companies must think it works. If they didn't, they wouldn't spend all that money!

The Basics of Advertising

Why would companies spend so much money to advertise to you? One reason is that many big companies or corporations have done their own research. Companies pay for market research companies to ask people what they buy, why, and where they buy their products. Companies have found that if people start buying a certain product when they are young, then they often stick with the same product throughout their lives. This is called brand loyalty. Brand loyalty is important to corporations because research has shown that if people are happy with the product they are using, it is very difficult to make them try a new product. The company that makes one kind of toothpaste wants people to use their product—even though they're quite happy with their usual brand. So lots of advertising is aimed at making people change their brand loyalty. Many television commercials compare two brands of the same product and say that one is better than the other. This is called comparative advertising and it's an attempt by the

company to change brand loyalty. It's a bit like comparison shopping, but the company is the one telling you what to believe.

There's another simple reason why companies and corporations want your attention—you have money to spend. Young people age five to fourteen buy about $16.7 billion worth of food, drinks, toys, and videos every year (and each year they spend more and more). That's a big market for companies, and they want your money! When you see or hear a commercial, think about what it is saying. Is there a famous person advertising the product? (The company wants you to think that by having the product you'll be as cool as the star.) Does the advertisement use music by bands that are popular with you and your friends? (They're trying to attract your attention to the product.) Are there people your age in the advertisement? Is everyone smiling as they use the product? (The company is trying to convince you that buying the product will make you and your friends happy.) If it's a toy commercial, what is it *not* saying about the toy? Do you need other things to make it work? Listen for phrases such as "batteries not included" or "some assembly required." Does the advertisement tell you everything you need to know about the product? If you're interested in the product, check it against ratings and reviews (see chapter 4).

There is another way that companies try to convince you to buy their stuff—it's called product placement. This means that companies pay television and film companies to show their products in a show or a film. Often this is very subtle. You might not even notice it at first, but once you know it's happening you'll start to see it everywhere. A character in a TV show might have a poster for a soon-to-be-released film in his bedroom, or another character might wear only one brand of clothes in a film.

So stay alert and think about the information you're being given. Separate fact from what companies want you to believe (which is often fiction). That way you'll never get fooled by an advertisement—and on top of that, you'll drive companies crazy trying to work out new ways to make you buy stuff!

Ethical Shopping

Even though most of us realize that we are living in a world of limited resources, sometimes we do not stop to really think about it. There are many reasons that we buy products that use lots of resources—maybe because they are cool or because they are particularly useful. We sometimes look at the cost only in terms of its immediate cost—how much money it takes to buy the product.

Social and Environmental Costs

But there is another way of looking at the cost, one that takes into account a product's environmental and social costs. To an economist, an economic good is simply something that improves the health of the economy—even if it is only in the short term. If a country cuts down its rain forest to sell the wood, to an economist this is a good thing. Trees that make no money standing up can make money once they are cut down. The sale of the wood will improve the country's economic output, and there will be more jobs and money for people.

But there are other costs besides the economic ones. Perhaps there will be flooding elsewhere in the country because there are fewer trees to absorb rainwater (an environmental cost). Maybe people who lived in the forest will have to move and find jobs and a life elsewhere (a social cost). Maybe to you an economic good is something different. You might, for example, think that it is better to keep the rain forest intact and find another, less costly, way to improve the country's economy.

Ethical shopping is about buying goods and services that take into account the social and environmental costs of producing them. It could be bananas grown without the use of chemicals that run off into rivers, or a bank that promises not to invest money in tobacco companies. You can do research to find out which companies act in a socially responsible way. For example, some clothing companies have factories in developing countries where workers are badly treated and sometimes paid as little as one cent an hour. The National Labor Coalition has lots of information that shows how much different clothing companies pay their workers and how the workers are treated. To find online stores that are aware of the costs of consuming, try *http://www.shopforchange.com*. The site will also tell you about ethical telephone companies and banks.

Speak Up!

If after doing some research you find that a company from which you buy products is acting in a way you don't like, write to them. Tell them if you don't like their trading or labor practices. You could even tell them that you will not buy their products until they change. Companies admit that public pressure (such as letter-writing campaigns) is a very effective way of making them change their practices. For example, in the 1980s tuna fish companies promised that they would sell only tuna that had been caught without killing dolphins, after thousands of people wrote to them saying that they would stop buying tuna if they didn't.

All of this goes to show once again that when you're shopping, whether it's for goods or for services, there is one thing that will give you more power than anything else. It's not having all the money you want—it's having all the knowledge you need. If you know what to look out for, then you will always be one step ahead.

GLOSSARY

advertisement A public announcement about a good or a service that tries to persuade you to buy that particular good or service.

barter A system of exchanging goods and services that does not involve money.

budget An estimate of how much you will save and spend in a certain period of time.

ethical shopping Buying goods and services that take into account their social and environmental cost, rather than just their economic cost.

opportunity cost An economist's way of saying cost; what you have to give up in order to have what you want.

product placement A practice in which companies pay for their products or services to be featured in a television show or film.

FOR MORE INFORMATION

Web Sites

Adbusters

http://www.adbusters.org
This Canadian organization creates a collection of spoof advertisements (called subvertisements) and sponsors an annual "Buy Nothing Day."

Allowance Net

http://www.allowance.net
This site uses virtual money called Diditz to help you learn about saving.

Big Money Adventure

http://www.agedwards.com/bma/index.shtml
This site includes games and stories that teach you about investing money and picking stocks.

Biz Rate

http://www.bizrate.com
This site will comparison shop for you, finding the cheapest price available.

I Can Buy

http://www.icanbuy.com
This site will tell you how to make the most of your money.

Kidsense

http://www.kidsenseonline.com
A community service program that is dedicated to improving kids' understanding of major concepts in the world of finance, including buying and selling, working and earning, and investing and saving.

National Labor Coalition

www.nlc.org
Discover how different clothing and shoe manufacturers treat workers in their overseas factories.

Save Lab

http://www.plan.ml.com/family/kids
Encourages kids and their families to come up with creative ways to save.

Statistics Canada

http://www.statcan.ca
An excellent source of statistics on Canadian government finances, revenues, and federal spending.

Young Investors Network

http://www.salomonsmithbarney.com/yin
Offers a free personalized plan to help you set and meet your financial goals.

The Young Investor Web Site

http://www.younginvestor.com/pick.shtml
A fun site that includes a stock market simulation game where you can research stocks and learn strategies for buying and selling them.

FOR FURTHER READING

Bangs, David H., Jr., and Linda Pinson. *The Real World Entrepreneur Field Guide*. New York: Upstart Press, 1999.

The Economist Guide to Economic Indicators: Making Sense of Economics. New York: John Wiley & Sons, 1997.

Giesbrecht, Martin Gerhard, and Gary E. Clayton. *A Guide to Everyday Economic Thinking*. New York: McGraw-Hill, 1997.

Godfrey, Neale S. *Neale S. Godfrey's Ultimate Kids' Money Book*. New York: Simon & Schuster, 1998.

Heilbroner, Robert, and Lester Thurow. *Economics Explained*. New York: Simon & Schuster, 1994.

Lee, Susan. *Susan Lee's ABZs of Economics*. New York: Pocket Books, 1987.

Mariotti, Steve (with Tony Towle and Debra DeSalvo). *The Young Entrepreneur's Guide to Starting and Running a Small Business*. New York: Random House, 1996.

Mastrianna, Frank V., and Thomas J. Hailstones. *Basic Economics*. South-Western College Publishing, 1998.

INDEX

INDEX

CREDITS

About the Author

Tom Ridgway lives and works in Paris, France, where a Big Mac costs French Francs 18.50, or 2.80 Euros.

Photo Credits

Cover photos © Artville; p. 7 © Michael S. Yamashita/Corbis; p. 10 © Paul A. Souders/Corbis; pp. 12, 33 © VCG/FPG; p. 20 © Jennie Woodcock, Reflections Photolibrary/Corbis; p. 27 © Hal Kern/International Stock Photography; p. 28 © Superstock; p. 30 © Telegraph Photo Library; p. 37 © Charles O'Rear/Corbis; p. 40 © Haroldo Castro/FPG.

Series Design

Law Alsobrook

Layout

Cynthia Williamson